THE TENETS
(Taekw(

The tenets of Taekwon-Do should ｜   d
live their lives.

COURTESY	**YE UI**
INTEGRITY	**TOM CHI**
PERSEVERANCE	**IN NAE**
SELF-CONTROL	**GUK GI**
INDOMITABLE SPIRIT	**BAEKJUL BOOLGOOL**

EXPLANATION OF TENETS

COURTESY
1) To promise the spirit of mutual concessions
2) To be ashamed of one's vices and contempt those of other's
3) Be polite to each other
4) Encourage the sense of justice
5) To distinguish the instructor from student and senior from junior

INTEGRITY
Be able to assume right from wrong and feel guilt when appropriate. The following are examples of a lack of integrity:
1) The instructor who teaches improper technique due to a lack of knowledge
2) A student who fixes breaking materials before demonstrations
3) The instructor who masks bad technique with luxurious facilities
4) The students who requests or purchases rank
5) The presence of ego relating to achieved rank
6) The instructor who concentrates more on profit than on student welfare and ability

PERSEVERANCE
Persistence in doing something despite delay or difficulty in achieving success. One must be able to persevere through many peaks and troughs on the journey from white to black belt to achieve technique and overcome hard times.

SELF CONTROL

One must master their self-control in order to be distinguished as a martial artist from a fighter. Taekwon-Do techniques can be dangerous and treated with respect. Losing control whilst sparring could prove disastrous.

INDOMITABLE SPIRIT

One who is unable to be dominated. This is the ability to proceed with a task and never give up regardless of how impossible the task seems. Consider those who achieve world records or climb the highest mountains and succeed against the odds.

TAEKWON-DO OATH AND DOJANG RULES

STUDENT OATH

1) I shall observe the tenets of Taekwon-Do
2) I shall respect my instructors and seniors
3) I shall never misuse Taekwon-Do
4) I shall be a champion of freedom and justice
5) I shall build a more peaceful world

RULES OF THE DOJANG (training hall)

1) All students must bow when entering or leaving the training hall when a black belt is present.
2) Prior to class all students should bow to black belts who enter the dojang, including black belts to their senior grades.
3) Students should bow before speaking to the instructor. Hands should be raised before speaking to attract the instructor's attention
4) Do not address your instructor by their first name. SIR/ MISS or MR/ MISS/ MRS [SURNAME] are appropriate.
5) Do not wear shoes in the dojang or during training unless permission has been given.
6) Do not chat idly during training. Focus and concentration should be maintained.
7) When lining up in class the senior grade in each line should be to the right of the dojang with equal numbers of people in each row. Students should stand behind someone from the second row backwards.
8) Students who arrive late should wait by the side of the dojang training area to be invited into the class by their instructor, who may request a reason for lateness.
9) If a student does not train for over one month they may be asked to carry out a reassessment grading.
10) Doboks (training uniforms) must be clean and PRESSED before every training session.

STUDENTS
(Jeja)

Never tire of learning. You should be able to train at any time, anywhere if required whether it be practical or theoretical.

Be prepared to sacrifice for their art and instructor. Whilst it is true that students purchase instruction with their money it is also expected to 'pitch in' with looking after training areas, helping fellow students, demonstrations and other duties.

Higher grades should always set a good example to younger students and those with lower belt rank. Junior grades will emulate higher grades.

Exercise loyalty. Do not unduly criticise the instructor, Taekwon-Do or teaching methods.

When your instructor teaches a technique, practise it and try to use it.

Maintain good conduct outside the dojang as well as inside. You represent your club at all times as well as your instructor and your art.

If a student adopts a technique from another dojang and the instructor disapproves of it, the student must discard it immediately or train at the gym where the technique was learned.

Do not be disrespectful to your instructor (or colleagues). Students are encouraged to question techniques for the purpose of understanding but should eventually follow the instructor's direction once justified.

Be eager to learn and ask questions.

Never break a trust.

GRADING SYSTEM AND BELT COLOURS

After a certain amount of time the student may apply to undertake a belt grading test. This is at the recommendation of the instructor and passes are never guaranteed.

COLOURED BELT GRADES

10th kup	WHITE BELT
9th kup	WHITE BELT/ YELLOW TAG
8th kup	YELLOW BELT
7th kup	YELLOW BELT/ GREEN TAG
6th kup	GREEN BELT
5th kup	GREEN BELT/ BLUE TAG
4th kup	BLUE BELT
3rd kup	BLUE BELT/ RED TAG
2nd kup	RED BELT
1st kup	RED BELT/ BLACK TAG

BLACK BELT RANKING

Achieving a black belt should be seen not as the end of the journey but rather the start of a new journey. A black belt should be considered as knowing the basics of Taekwon-Do and be able to defend themselves against a single opponent effectively.

1ST DEGREE	
2ND DEGREE	NOVICE
3RD DEGREE	
4TH DEGREE	
5TH DEGREE	EXPERT
6TH DEGREE	
7TH DEGREE	
8TH DEGREE	MASTER
9TH DEGREE	

THE EXPLANATION OF BELT COLOURS

WHITE   Signifies innocence as that of the beginning student who has no previous knowledge of Taekwon-Do.

YELLOW   Signifies earth from which the plant takes root and sprouts as Taekwon-Do foundations are laid.

GREEN   Signifies the plant's growth as Taekwon-Do skills begin to develop.

BLUE   Signifies the heaven towards which the plant matures into a towering tree as training in Taekwon-Do progresses.

RED   Signifies danger, cautioning the student to exercise control and warning the opponent to stay away.

BLACK   Opposite of white, therefore signifies maturity and proficiency in Taekwon-Do. It also indicates the wearers imperviousness to darkness and fear.

TITLE AND FUNCTION

The various levels of black belt have different titles which should be used when addressing a black belt. Using the correct title is clear understanding of the time and effort that has been taken by that individual to achieve their rank.

Master status in ITF Taekwon-Do is achieved at 7th degree black belt and not 4th degree. This title requires expertise to back up the title and falsely claiming a master rank at a grade lower than 7th degree black belt belittles our art.

Degree holders should use the appropriate titles:

1st to 3rd degree	**BOOSABUM** Assistant Instructor (when necessary)
4th to 6th degree	**SABUM** Instructor
7th to 8th degree	**SAHYUN** Master
9th degree	**SASUNG** Grand Master

To commence class, the senior student would say:

CHARYOT (attention), **SABUM NIMGEH** (Respect for instructor), **KYONG YE** (Bow)

PATTERNS

A pattern (tul) is a series of fundamental movements, most of which represent and attack or defence against an imaginary opponent set to a fixed or logical sequence.

The tul form a practical 'catalogue' of the fundamental movements in Taekwon-Do. For this reason it is important to study not just the sequence and technicalities of each movement but also the application and use of them.

By going through a variety of movements the student is able to practice combinations which may be used during sparring or confrontation which improving flexibility, fitness and technique.

There are a total of 24 patterns in ITF Taekwon-Do.

THE REASON FOR 24 PATTERNS

THE LIFE OF A HUMAN BEING, PERHAPS 100 YEARS, CAN BE CONSIDERED AS A DAY WHEN COMPARED WITH ETERNITY. THEREFORE, WE MORTALS ARE NO MORE THAN SIMPLE TRAVELLERS WHO PASS BY THE ETERNAL YEARS OF AN EON IN A DAY.

IT IS EVIDENT THAT NO ONE CAN LIVE MORE THAN A LIMITED AMOUNT OF TIME. NEVERTHELESS, MOST PEOPLE FOOLISHLY ENSLAVE THEMSELVES TO MATERIALISM AS IF THEY COULD LIVE FOR THOUSANDS OF YEARS. AND SOME PEOPLE STRIVE TO BEQUEATH A GOOD SPIRITUAL LEGACY FOR COMING GENERATIONS, IN THIS WAY, GAINING IMMORTALITY. OBVIOUSLY, THE SPIRIT IS PERPETUAL WHILE MATERIAL IS NOT. THEREFORE, WHAT WE CAN DO TO LEAVE BEHIND SOMETHING FOR THE WELFARE OF MANKIND IS, PERHAPS, THE MOST IMPORTANT THING IN OUR LIVES.

THE DIAGRAM OF A PATTERN

THIS IS A DIAGRAM WHICH CAN BE LAID OUT ON THE FLOOR AS A 'DIRECTIONAL MAP' OF THE PATTERN. PATTERNS SHOULD START AND FINISH ON THE SAME SPOT AND SO DIAGRAMS ARE IMPORTANT AND MUST BE FOLLOWED CLOSELY.

COLOURED BELT PATTERNS

9th kup	CHON JI
8th kup	DAN GUN
7th kup	DO SAN
6th kup	WON HYO
5th kup	YUL GOK
4th ku	JOONG GUN
3rd kup	TOI GYE
2nd kup	HWA RANG
1st kup	CHOONG MOO

BLACK BELT PATTERNS

1ST DEGREE	KWANG GAE PO EUN GAE BAEK
2ND DEGREE	EUI AM CHOON JANG JUCHE
3RD DEGREE	SAM IL YOO SIN CHOI YONG
4TH DEGREE	YONG GAE UL JI MOON MOO
5TH DEGREE	SO SAN SE JONG
6TH DEGREE	TONG IL

		CHARYOT	ATTENTION
HANA	ONE	KYONG YE	BOW
DUL	TWO	JUNBI	READY
SET	THREE	SI JAK	START
NEY	FOUR	GOMAN	STOP
TASUT	FIVE	HAECHYO	BREAK
YASUT	SIX	TIRO TORO	TURN AROUND
ILGOP	SEVEN	NAGAGI	FORWARD
YADUL	EIGHT	DURUOGI	BACKWARD
AHOP	NINE	BARO	RETURN
YAUL	TEN	SWIYO	RELAX
		HAESAN	CLASS DISMISSED

WORDS USED IN THE DOJANG (ABOVE) & STANCES (BELOW)

CHARYOT SOGI	ATTENTION STANCE
NARANI SOGI	PARALLEL STANCE
ANNUN SOGI	SITTING STANCE
GUNNUN SOGI	WALKING STANCE
NIUNJA SOGI	L STANCE
GOJUNG SOGI	FIXED STANCE
GOBURYU SOGI	BENDING STANCE
KYOCHA SOGI	X STANCE
DWITBAL SOGI	REAR FOOT STANCE
NACHUO SOGI	LOW STANCE
SOO JIK SOGI	VERTICAL STANCE
SASUN SOGI	DIAGONAL STANCE
MOOSA SOGI	WARRIOR STANCE
WAEBAL SOGI	ONE LEG STANCE
OGURYO SOGI	CROUCHED STANCE
PALJA SOGI	OPEN STANCE

ATTACKING AND BLOCKING TOOLS

HAND PARTS	**SANG BANSIN**	**FOREARM PARTS**	
FOREFIST	**AP JOOMUK**	OUTER FOREARM	**BAKAT PALMOK**
BACKFIST	**DUNG JOOMUK**	INNER FOREARM	**AN PALMOK**
SIDEFIST	**YOP JOOMUK**	BACK FOREARM	**DUNG PALMOK**
UNDERFIST	**MIT JOOMUK**	UNDER FOREARM	**MIT PALMOK**
PALM	**SONBADAK**		
MIDDLE KNUCKLE FIST	**JONGJI JOOMUK**		
FORE KNUCKLE FIST	**INJI JOOMUK**	**ELBOW PARTS**	
KNIFEHAND	**SONKAL**	BACK ELBOW	**DWIT PALKUP**
REVERSE KNIFEHAND	**SONKAL DUNG**	SIDE ELBOW	**YOP PALKUP**
THUMB	**OMJI SONGARAK**	DOUBLE SIDE ELBOW	**JAU PALKUP**
FOREFINGER	**HAN SONGARAK**	STRAIGHT ELBOW	**SUN PALKUP**
DOUBLE FOREFINGER	**DOO SONGARAK**	UPPER ELBOW	**WI PALKUP**
FLAT FINGERTIP	**OPUN SONKUT**	FRONT ELBOW	**AP PALKUP**
ANGLE FINGERTIP	**HOMI SONKUT**	HIGH ELBOW	**NOPUN**
STRAIGHT FINGERTIP	**SUN SONKUT**		**PALKUP**
UPSET FINGERTIP	**DWIJIBUN SONKUT**		
ARC HAND	**BANDALSON**		
BACKHAND	**SONDUNG**		
FINGERBELLY	**SONGARAK BADAK**		
LONG FIST	**GHIN JOOMUK**		
OPEN FIST	**RYUN JOOMUK**		

FOOT PARTS	
BALL OF FOOT	**AP KUMCHI**
BACK SOLE	**DWIKUMCHI**
FOOTSWORD	**BALKAL**
BACK HEEL	**DWICHOOK**
INSTEP	**BALDUNG**
SIDE SOLE	**YOP BAL BADAK**
REVERSE FOOTSWORD	**BALKAL DUNG**

HAND PARTS – **SANG BANSIN**

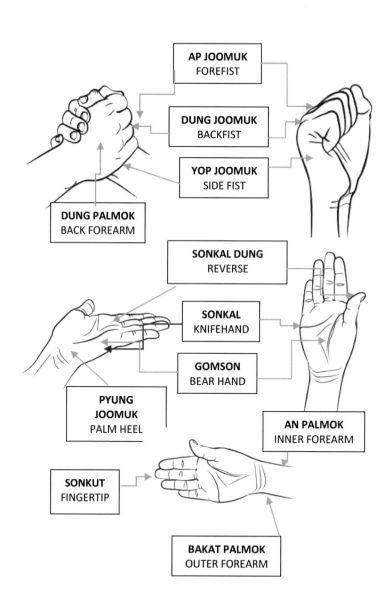

AP JOOMUK
FOREFIST

DUNG JOOMUK
BACKFIST

YOP JOOMUK
SIDE FIST

DUNG PALMOK
BACK FOREARM

SONKAL DUNG
REVERSE

SONKAL
KNIFEHAND

GOMSON
BEAR HAND

PYUNG JOOMUK
PALM HEEL

AN PALMOK
INNER FOREARM

SONKUT
FINGERTIP

BAKAT PALMOK
OUTER FOREARM

HAND TECHNIQUES
Son Gisool

Hand techniques are fundamental in application of blocking and care should be taken to adhere to correct principles during execution.

COMMON PRINCIPLES:

1) The hips turn in the same direction and with the attacking or blocking tool from the start to the finish of the movement.
2) When performing spot techniques raise the heel at the start of the movement and place firmly on the ground at the point of execution.
3) Raise the body at the beginning of the movement and lower it at the point of impact (adhere to sine wave)
4) Hand movements start with a backwards motion to exploit maximum velocity.
5) Whilst the movement is executed both arms should be slightly bent.

ATTACKING TECHNIQUES
Gong Gyoki

Attacking can be made by punching, striking and thrusting as well as pressing, breaking and cross cutting. The principles of the motions of the first three of these need to be understood:

1) **A PUNCH** is used primarily to cause an internal haemorrhage by twisting the attacking tool at the point of impact.
2) **A THRUST** involves less twisting motion than a punch and is designed to cut through the target
3) **A STRIKE** involves the least twisting motion of the attacking tool and is designed to destroy or break bone or muscle at the vital point of the target.

FOOT TECHNIQUES
Bal Gisool

ATTACK TECHNIQUES (**GONG GYOK GI**)

FRONT SNAP KICK	**AP CHA BUSIGI**
SIDE/FRONT SNAP KICK	**YOPAP CHA BUSIGI**
TURNING KICK	**DOLLYO CHAGI**
SIDE TURNING KICK	**YOP DOLLYO CHAGI**
SIDE PIERCING KICK	**YOP CHA JIRUGI**
SIDE THRUSTING KICK	**YOP CHA TULGI**
SIDE PUSHING KICK	**YOP CHA MILGI**
BACK PIERCING KICK	**DWITCHA JIRUGI**
BACK PUSHING KICK	**DWITCHA MILGI**
BACK SNAP KICK	**DWITCHA BUSIGI**
REVERSE TURNING KICK	**BANDAE DOLLYO CHAGI**
REVERSE HOOKING KICK	**BANDAE DOLLYO GORO CHAGI**
DOWNWARD KICK	**NAERYO CHAGI**
PICK SHAPED KICK	**GOK KAENGI CHAGI**
PRESSING KICK	**NOOLLO CHAGI**
TWISTING KICK	**BITURO CHAGI**
SWEEPING KICK	**SUROH CHAGI**
STAMPING KICK	**CHA BAPGI**
VERTICAL KICK	**SEWO CHAGI**
FLYING KICK	**TWIMYO CHAGI**
MID AIR KICK	**TWIO DOLMYO CHAGI**
OVERHEAD KICK	**TWIO NOMO CHAGI**
CONSECUTIVE KICK	**YONSOK CHAGI**
TWO DIRECTION KICK	**SANG BANG CHAGI**
FLYING DOUBLE KICK	**TWIMYO I-JUNG CHAGI**
FLYING TRIPLE KICK	**TWIMYO SAMJUNG CHAGI**

DEFENCE TECHNIQUES (**BANG EAU-GI**)

FRONT RISING KICK	**AP CHA OLLIGI**	DODGING	**PIHAGI**
SIDE RAISING KICK	**YOP CHA OLLIGI**	SLIDING	**MIKULGI**
CRESCENT KICK	**BANDAL CHAGI**	TURNING	**DOLGI**
HOOKING KICK	**GOLCHO CHAGI**	JUMPING	**TWIGI**
WAVING KICK	**DORO CHAGI**	FOOT LIFTING	**BAL DULGI**
FRONT CHECKING KICK	**APCHA MOMCHAGI**	BODY DROP	**MOM NACHUGI**
SIDE CHECKING KICK	**YOP CHA MOMCHAGI**	STEPPING	**OMGYO DIDIGI**

FOOT PARTS- **HABANSIN**

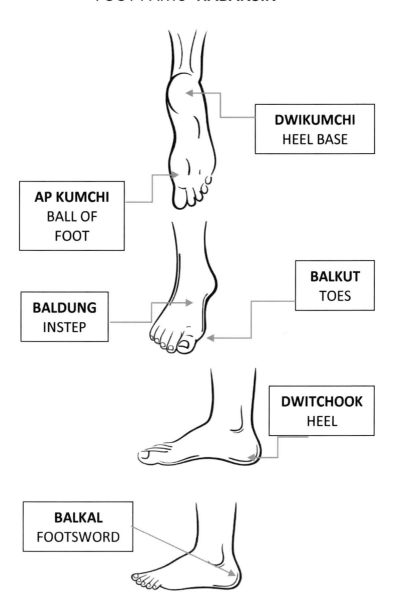

DWIKUMCHI
HEEL BASE

AP KUMCHI
BALL OF
FOOT

BALKUT
TOES

BALDUNG
INSTEP

DWITCHOOK
HEEL

BALKAL
FOOTSWORD

SECTIONS OF THE BODY

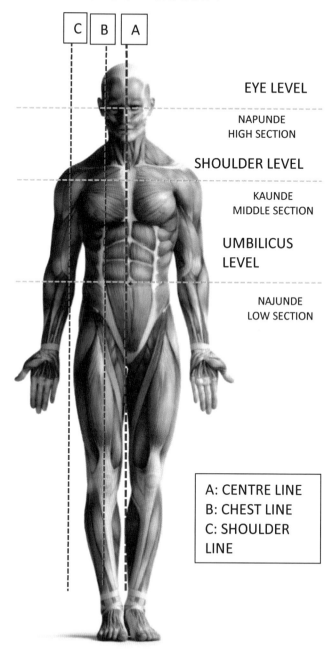

C B A

EYE LEVEL

NAPUNDE
HIGH SECTION

SHOULDER LEVEL

KAUNDE
MIDDLE SECTION

UMBILICUS
LEVEL

NAJUNDE
LOW SECTION

A: CENTRE LINE
B: CHEST LINE
C: SHOULDER
LINE

STANCES
SOGI

The stance is the starting point for all techniques. The feet connect with the ground which is ultimately where the power starts from. Stances must be correct to allow proper body alignments and enable the student to improve stability, agility, balance and flexibility.

PRINCIPLES FOR A CORRECT STANCE:
KEEP THE BACK STRAIGHT (WITH FEW EXCEPTIONS)
KEEP THE SHOULDERS RELAXED
TENSE THE ABDOMEN
MAINTAIN CORRECT FACING (FULL, HALF OR SIDE FACING)
MAINTAIN EQUILIBRIUM (BALANCE)
MAKE CORRECT USE OF KNEE SPRING

ATTENTION STANCE (CHARYOT SOGI)

THIS IS THE POSITION USED BEFORE STARTING AN EXERCISE

45 DEGREE ANGLE BETWEEN THE FEET
HEELS TOGETHER
FISTS HANG NATURALLY WITH ELBOWS SLIGHTLY BENT
EYES FACE FROM SLIGHTLY ABOVE HORIZONTAL LINE

BOW POSTURE (KYONG YE JASE)

WHILST MAINTAINING CHARYOT SOGI:

BEND THE BODY 15 FORWARDS
MAINTAIN STRAIGHT BACK
KEEP EYES FIXED ON OPPONENT'S EYES

PARALLEL STANCE (NARANI SOGI)

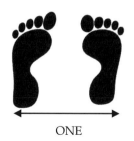

SPREAD FEET TO SHOULDER WIL
TOES POINT FORWARDS
CAN BE FULL OR SIDE FACING
50/50 WEIGHT DISTRIBUTION

ONE

WALKING STANCE (GUNNUN SOGI)

STRONG STANCE FRONT & REAR.
MOVE ONE FOOT FORWARD OR
BACKWARD TO A DISTANCE OF 1.5
SHOULDER WIDTHS BETWEEN BIG TOES.
INCREASING THIS DISTANCE WEAKENS
THE STANCE.
BEND THE FRONT LEG SO THAT THE KNEE
IS OVER THE HEEL
KEEP BACK LEG STRAIGHT.
BODYWEIGHT IS DISTRIBUTED EVENLY
OVER BOTH FEET.
TOES OF FRONT FOOT POINT FORWARDS.
TOES OF BACK FOOT POINT NO MORE
THAN 25 DEGREES OUTWARDS.
TENSE FOOT MUSCLES GRIPPING THE
GROUND WITH TOES.
CAN BE FULL OR HALF FACING.

A RIGHT WALKING STANCE HAS THE
RIGHT FOOT FORWARD AND VICE VERSA.

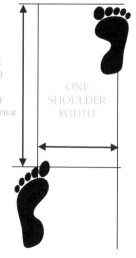

ONE AND A HALF SHOULDER

ONE SHOULDER WIDTH

SITTING STANCE (ANNUN SOGI)

STABLE STANCE FROM SIDE TO SIDE AND
IS A USEFUL STANCE TO PRACTICE
PUNCHING, SIDE KICKS AND
STRENGTHENING THE LEG MUSCLES.

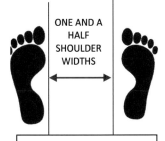

ONE AND A HALF SHOULDER WIDTHS

    MOVE ONE FOOT TO THE SIDE AT A
    DISTANCE OF 1.5 SHOULDER
    WIDTHS.
    POINT TOES FORWARDS.
    WEIGHT DISTRIBUTION IS EVEN
    OVER BOTH FEET.
    BEND KNEES UNTIL KNEE IS OVER
    BALL OF FOOT.
    DO NOT LET KNEES COLLAPSE. GRIP
    FLOOR WITH OUTSIDE OF FEET.
    PULL HIPS BACK AND TENSE
    ABDOMEN AND LOWER BACK

WIDENING THE FEET
MORE THAN 1.5
SHOULDER WIDTHS
WEAKEN THE
STRUCTURE OF THE
STANCE AND INHIBIT
MOVEMENT. STANCE
CAN BE FULL OR SIDE
FACING IN BOTH ATTACK
AND DEFENCE.

L STANCE (NIUNJA SOGI)

USEFUL AS A DEFENCE STANCE WITH ATTACK
APPLICATION TOO. FRONT FOOT IS AVAILABLE
TO KICK.

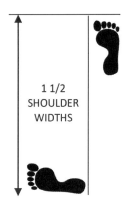

1 1/2 SHOULDER WIDTHS

    MOVE ONE FOOT FORWARDS OR
    BACKWARDS TO A DISTANCE OF 1.5
    SHOULDER WIDTHS FROM REAR
    FOOTSWORD TO FRONT BIG TOE.
    TOES OF BOTH FEET TURN 15 DEGREES
    INWARDS.
    FRONT HEEL IS 2.5CM BEYOND REAR
    HEEL FOR STABILITY.
    KEEP HIPS ALIGNED WITH INNER KNEE

FIXED STANCE (GOJUN SOGI)

SIMILAR TO L STANCE THIS STANCE IS EFFECTIVE FOR ATTACK AND DEFENCE TO THE SIDE. AS L STANCE BUT WITH THE FOLLOWING AMENDMENTS:

50/50 WEIGHT DISTRIBUTION.
DISTSNCE BETWEEN BOTH BIG TOES IS 1.5 SHOULDER WIDTHS
WHEN RIGHT FOOT IS FORWARD STANCE IS A RIGHT STANCE AND VICE VERSA

VERTICAL STANCE (**SOOJIK SOGI**)

MOVE ONE FOOT TO FRONT OR SIDE SO THAT DISTANCE BETWEEN BIG TOES IS 1 SHOULDER WIDTH
60% WEIGHT ON REAR FOOT. 40% ON FRONT FOOT.
TOES SHOULD POINT 15 DEGREES INWARDS
LEGS SHOULD BE STRAIGHT

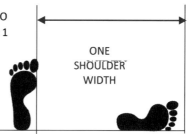

THE REAR FOOT DENOTES THE STANCE. RIGHT FOOT AT THE BACK IS A RIGHT VERTICAL STANCE AND VICE VERSA. THIS STANCE IS ALWAYS HALF FACING WHETHER IN ATTACK OR DEFENCE.

REAR FOOT STANCE (DWITBAL SOGI)

MAINLY A DEFENSIVE STANCE. THE FRONT FOOT IS QUICKLY ADAPTABLE TO ATTACK OR DEFEND/ CHECK DISTANCE FROM OPPONENT. NO SHIFTING OF WEIGHT IS REQUIRED FOR FRONT FOOT TECHNIQUES

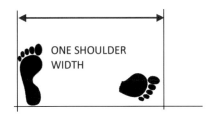

MOVE ONE FOOT FORWARD OR BACKWARDS SO THAT THERE IS ONE SHOULDER WIDTH BETWEEN REAR FOOT BALKAL AND FRONT FOOT BIG TOE
REAR LEG SHOULD BE BEND WITH KNEE OVER TOES.
FRONT LEG SHOULD BEND WITH ONLY FRONT HALF OF FOOT ON FLOOR
REAR HEEL SHOULD BE SLIGHTLY BEYOND FRONT HEEL
FRONT FOOT TOES POINT INWARDS 25 DEGREES INWARDS AND REAR TOES 15 DEGREES INWARDS.
MOST OF THE BODYWEIGHT IS SUPPORTED BY THE REAR FOOT.

THE REAR FOOT DENOTES WHETHER STUDENT IS IN A LEFT OR RIGHT STANCE.

BENDING STANCE (GOBURYO SOGI)

THIS IS A PREPARATORY STANCE FOR SIDE AND BACK KICKS.

STUDENT WILL STAND ON ONE FOOT WITH KNEE SLIGHTLY BENT.

THE FOOT ON THE FLOOR DENOTES LEFT OR RIGHT STANCE

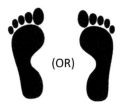

CAN BE EITHER FULL OR HALF FACING.

X STANCE (**KYOCHA SOGI**)

CONVENIENT STANCE USED
FOR GAINING DISTANCE
AND ATTACKING THE SIDE
OR FRONT WITH A JUMP.
THIS STANCE IS OFTEN USED
WHILST BLOCKING AND AS
A TRANSITIONARY STANCE.

CROSS ONE FOOTBEHIND THE OTHER AND TOUCH THE GROUND LIGHTLY
WITH THE BALL OF THAT FOOT.
PLACE BODYWEIGHT ON THE OTHER FOOT WHICH IS COMPLETELY ON
THE FLOOR

LOW STANCE (**NACHUO SOGI**)

LOW STANCE SERVES TO GAIN
EXTRA DISTANCE TOWARDS THE
OPPONENT THEREBY
LENGTHENING THE ATTACKING
TOOL. IT WILL BUILD LEG
MUSCLES.

LOW STANCE IS SIMILAR TO
WALKING STANCE BUT IT IS
LONGER BY ONE FOOT.

IT CAN BE EITHER FULL OR HALF
FACING.

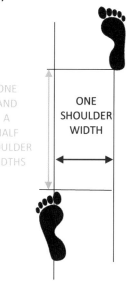

ONE
AND
A
HALF
SHOULDER
WIDTHS

ONE
SHOULDER
WIDTH

SPARRING (**MATSOGI**)

THREE STEP SPARRING (**SAMBO MATSOGI**)

This is the most basic of sparring exercises and is generally used in grading from 9th to 6th kup. It serves as a means to become familiar with simple blocks and attacks at either high, middle or low section against an opponent whilst stepping backwards or forwards.

TWO STEP SPARRING (**IBO MATSOGI**)

The purpose of two step sparring is to combine hand and foot attacks and defences. The attacker must use the hand and foot alternatively. It is up to the attacker to choose which to use first. Attackers should measure up accordingly before each attack and defender should counter attack after second defence.

ONE STEP SPARRING (**ILBO MATSOGI**)

One aim of Taekwon-Do is to achieve victory in one single blow. For this reason one step sparring is seen as a giant step towards this objective and the most important of the three sparring exercises mentioned thus far.

Students should face each other in junbi stance and acknowledge that their partner is ready using 'kiup'. It is from this position that the attacker will start their attack using a punch on both the right and then the left side. The defender will need to choose a defence and counter attack using a variety of techniques as required. The secret to one step sparring is to deliver an accurately timed blow to the opponent's vital spot whilst defending the opponent's attack.

SEMI FREE SPARRING (**BAN JAYOO MATSOGI**)

This is the last stage of sparring before the student enters into completely free sparring. All movements, distance and use of attacking and defending tools are optional. Only one series of attack and defence motions are exchanged and only for a brief duration.

FREE SPARRING (**JAYOO MATSOGI**)

Free sparring is open combat whilst exercising a certain level of control in the dojang. Nothing is pre-arranged during free sparring and students may attack and defend as they wish within the parameters of Taekwon-Do. Control must be exercised when attacking vital spots and protective equipment should be worn as level of contract increases.

PROMOTIONAL GRADINGS

Throughout the journey of the Taekwon-Do student grading tests will be carried out to distinguish what level has been achieved by the student. This way each student can recognise rank order within any class environment from white to black belt and from black belt to instructor.

The belt rank cannot be requested and is not given by time training alone. It is a reflection of the effort and dedication of the student not just during their grading but in the weeks and months leading up to it. For this reason students should ALWAYS be seen to be trying to improve their standards during training.

Certain criteria MUST be adhered to for the student to be accepted for a grading test:

1) THE STUDENT MUST BE OF THE REQUIRED STANDARD
2) THE STUDENT MUST HAVE A CLEAR UNDERSTANDING OF THEIR THEORY
3) THE BEHAVIOUR OF THE STUDENT MUST ALWAYS REPRESENT TO DOJANG, INSTRUCTOR AND COLLEAGUES TO THE HIGHEST LEVEL
4) THE STUDENT MUST ENSURE THAT THEIR REPRESENTATION OF THEIR ART, SCHOOL AND INSTRUCTOR MUST BE OF A HIGH STANDARD NOT JUST IN THE DOJANG BUT IN ALL WALKS OF THEIR LIFE.

Taekwon-Do is a martial art that can be practiced from a very young age to a very old age. It would be unfair to expect students of varying ages and abilities to undertake a blanket exam to pass a grading. Therefore it is typical to ask younger students less theory questions than adults and also not to expect older students to be as athletic as younger ones.

The grading system can be split into three categories:

1) JUNIOR GRADE
2) STANDARD GRADE
3) EXECUTIVE GRADE

The type of grade taken should mean that the challenge is equally as difficult for all ages and also a fair representation of individual ability.

GRADING REQUIREMENTS

GRADING ETIQUETTE

Promotional exams are formal grading exams and should be treated with respect accordingly. Standards are required to be kept high and rules need to be adhered to. The following is a list of basic requirements:

1) MANY PEOPLE IN A GRADING MAY MEAN PERIODS OF TIME WAITING. BE PREPARED TO SIT QUIETLY AND BE PATIENT.
2) YOUR DOBOK MUST BE CLEAN AND PRESSED.
3) YOUR BELT MUST BE TIED CORRECTLY
4) LICENSES SHOULD BE UP TO DATE
5) PAYMENTS MUST BE MADE ON TIME BEFORE YOU GRADE.
6) YOU SHOULD ENSURE YOU HAVE STUDIED ENOUGH TO PASS YOUR GRADING.

OTHER POINTS TO CONSIDER FOR YOUR FIRST GRADING:

1) YOUR INSTRUCTOR WILL NAME EACH TECHNIQUE IN ENGLISH AND KOREAN AND DEMONSTRATE THAT MOVEMENT FOR YOU TO COPY.
2) AS SOON AS YOU ENTER THE HALL YOU ARE BEING GRADED SO BEHAVE ACCORDINGLY. YOU WILL BOW ON ENTRY, LINE UP, BOW, RECITE TENETS AND OATH AND BE DISMISSED TO THE BACK OF THE ROOM WHERE YOU SHOULD SIT CROSS LEGGED UNTIL YOU ARE CALLED.
3) WHEN YOUR NAME IS CALLED YOU SHOULD MOVE TO THE ALLOCATED SPOT ON THE FLOOR AND INFORM THE EXAMINING INSTRUCTOR OF YOUR FULL NAME, RANK AND ADDRESS THEM AS SIR/ MISS.
4) THEORY WILL BE THE FINAL PART OF YOUR GRADING. YOU WILL BE CALLED TO THE EXAMINER'S TABLE. ALL QUESTIONS SHOULD BE ANSWERED COURTEOUSLY AND CONFIDENTLY. ONCE DISMISSED YOU MUSY BOW BEFORE YOU LEAVE AND TAKE THREE STEPS BACKWARDS BEFORE RETURNING TO YOUR SPOT. TURNING YOUR BACK ON AN INSTRUCTOR IS CONSIDERED DISCOURTEOUS.

10TH KUP TO 9TH KUP
GRADING SYLLABUS

PART 1: BASIC MOVEMENTS

SITTING STANCE, MIDDLE PUNCH
FRONT RISING KICK
WALKING STANCE, MIDDLE INNER FOREARM BLOCK
WALKING STANCE, LOW KNIFEHAND BLOCK
WALKING STANCE, LOW OUTER FOREARM BLOCK, REVERSE PUNCH
WALKING STANCE, MIDDLE INNER FOREARM BLOCK, REVERSE LOW OUTER FOREARM BLOCK

ANNUN SOGI, KAUNDE JIRUGI
AP CHA OLLIGI
GUNNUN SOGI, KAUNDE AN PALMOK MAKGI
GUNNUN SOGI, NAJUNDE SONKAL MAKGI
GUNNUN SOGI, NAJUNDE BAKAT PALMOK, MAKGI, BANDAE JIRUGI
GUNNUN SOGI, KAUNDE AN PALMOK MAKGI, BANDAE NAJUNDE BAKAT PALMOK MAKGI

PART 2: DIRECTIONAL EXERCISES

4 DIRECTIONAL PUNCH
WALKING STANCE, LOW OUTER FOREARM BLOCK
WALKING STANCE, MIDDLE PUNCH

SAJU JIRUGI
GUNNUN SOGI, NAJUNDE BAKAT PALMOK MAKGI
GUNNUN SOGI, KAUNDE JIRUGI

4 DIRECTIONAL BLOCK
WALKING STANCE, MIDDLE INNER FOREARM BLOCK
WALKING STANCE LOW KNIFEHAND BLOCK

SAJU MAKGI
GUNNUN SOGI, KAUNDE AN PALMOK MAKGI
GUNNUN SOGI, NAJUNDE SONKAL MAKGI

PART 3: TERMINOLOGY

HERE IS AN EXAMPLE OF COMMON QUESTIONS ASKED:

WHO IS THE FOUNDER OF TAEKWON-DO?
WHAT DOES TAEKWON-DO MEAN?
WHAT DOES WHITE SIGNIFY?
WHEN WAS TAEKWON-DO FOUNDED
NAME ANY BLOCKS, PUNCHES AND STANCES IN KOREAN LEARNED SO FAR.

9th KUP

PATTERN	**CHON JI**
NO. OF MOVEMENTS	**19**
READY POSITION	**NARANI JUNBI SOGI**

```
        C
        |
A ——————X—————— B
        |
        D   DIAGRAM
```

MEANING OF PATTERN

CHON JI literally means 'The Heaven, The Earth'
and is in the orient interpreted as the beginning
of the world and the creation of human history.
Therefore it is the initial pattern played by the beginning student.

It has two similar parts, one to represent the heaven and the other
the earth.

MOVEMENTS IN PATTERNS

STANCES	**SOGI**
WALKING STANCE	GUNNUN SOGI
L STANCE	NIUNJA SOGI

BLOCKS	**MAKGI**
LOW OUTER FOREARM BLOCK	NAJUNDE BAKAT PALMOK MAKGI
INNER FOREARM BLOCK	AN PALMOK MAKGI

PUNCHES	**JIRUGI**
MIDDLEPUNCH	KAUNDE JIRUGI

END	BRING LEFT FOOT BACK TO NARANI JUNBI SOGI

8TH KUP

PATTERN	DAN GUN	
NO. OF MOVEMENTS	21	
READY POSITION	NARANI JUNBI SOGI	

```
            C
            |
A —————————X————————— B
            |
            |
E —————————|————————— F
            D
```

MEANING OF PATTERN

DAN GUN is named after the Holy Dan Gun, the legendary founder of Korea in the year 2333 BC.

MOVEMENTS IN PATTERN

STANCES	SOGI
WALKING STANCE]	GUNNUN SOGI
L STANCE	NIUNJA SOGI

BLOCKS	MAKGI
OUTER FOREARM RISING BLOCK	BAKAT PALMOK CHOOKYO MAKGI
MIDDLE KNIFEHAND GUARDING BLOCK	KAUNDE SONKAL DAEBI MAKGI
LOW OUTER FOREARM BLOCK	NAJUNDE BAKAT PALMOK MAKGI
TWIN FOREARM BLOCK	SANG PALMOK MAKGI

PUNCHES	JIRUGI
HIGH PUNCH	NAPUNDE JIRUGI

STRIKE	TAERIGI
MIDDLE KNIFEHAND SIDE STRIKE	KAUNDE SONKAL YOP TAERIGI

END	
	BRING LEFT FOOT BACK TO NARANI CHUNBI SOGI

7th KUP

PATTERN

DO SAN

NO. OF MOVEMENTS

24

READY POSITION

NARANI JUNBI SOGI

```
              C
        A     X ──── B

        E ──── │    F
              D
```

MEANING OF PATTERN

DIAGRAM

DO SAN is the pseudonym of the patriot Ahn Chang Ho (1876 – 1938). The 24 movements represent his entire life which he dedicated to furthering the education of Korea and its independence movement.

MOVEMENTS IN PATTERN

STANCES
WALKING STANCE
L STANCE
SITTING STANCE

SOGI
GUNNUN SOGI
NIUNJA SOGI
ANNUN SOGI

BLOCKS
HIGH OUTER FOREARM WEDGING BLOCK

HIGH OUTER FOREARM SIDE BLOCK
OUTER FOREARM RISING BLOCK
MIDDLE KNIFEHAND GUARDING BLOCK

MAKGI
NAPUNDE BAKAT PALMOK HECHYO MAKGI
NAPUNDE BAKAT PALMOK MAKGI
BAKAT PALMOK CHOOKYO MAKGI
KAUNDE SONKAL DAEBI MAKGI

PUNCHES
MIDDLE PUNCH

JIRUGI
KAUNDE JIRUGI

STRIKES
MIDDLE KNIFEHAND SIDE STRIKE
HIGH BACKFIST SIDE STRIKE

TAERIGI
KAUNDE SONKAL YOP TAERIGI
NAPUNDE DUNG JOOMUK YOP TAERIGI

THRUST
MIDDLE STRAIGHT FINGERTIP THRUST

TULGI
KAUNDE SUN SONKUT TULGI

KICK
LOW FRONT SNAP KICK

CHAGI
NAJUNDE AP CHA BUSIGI

RELEASE FROM HOLD
END

JAPP YOSUL TAE
BRING RIGHT FOOT BACK TO NARANI CHUNBI SOGI

6th KUP

PATTERN	WON HYO
NO. OF MOVEMENTS	28
READY POSITION	MOA JUNBI SOGI A

```
            C
  A ————————X———————— B
            |
            |
  E ————————|———————— F
            D
```

DIAGRAM

MEANING OF PATTERN

WON HYO is named after the noted month Won Hyo who introduced Buddhism to the Silla Dynasty in the year 686 AD

STANCES
WALKING STANCE
L STANCE
CLOSE STANCE
BENDING READY STANCE A
FIXED STANCE

SOGI
GUNNUN SOGI
NIUNJA SOGI
MOA SOGI
GOBURYO JUNBI SOGI A
GOJUNG SOGI

BLOCKS
MIDDLE FOREARM GUARDING BLOCK
INNER FOREARM CICULAR BLOCK
TWIN FOREARM BLOCK
MIDDLE KNIFEHAND GUARDING BLOCK

MAKGI
KAUNDE PALMOK DAEBI MAKGI
AN PALMOK DOLLIMYO MAKGI
SANG PALMOK MAKGI
KAUNDE SONKAL DAEBI MAKGI

PUNCHES
MIDDLE PUNCH

JIRUGI
KAUNDE JIRUGI

STRIKE
HIGH INWARD KNIFEHAND STRIKE

TAERIGI
NAPUNDE ANNURO SONKAL MAKGI

THRUST
MIDDLE STRAIGHT FINGERTIP THRUST

TULGI
KAUNDE SUN SONKUT TULGI

KICK
LOW FRONT SNAP KICK
MIDDLE SIDE PIERCING KICK

CHAGI
NAJUNDE AP CHA BUSIGI
KAUNDE YOP CHA JIRUGI

END

BRING RIGHT FOOT BACK TO MOA SOGI A

THREE STEP SPARRING (SAMBO MATSOGI)

From 9th to 6th kup students will be expected to perform three step sparring for their grading tests to demonstrate basic ability in this field whilst stepping backwards and forward.

Attacks may be high, middle or lower levels as indicated by your instructor. The following are examples of three step sparring:

EXAMPLE 1
ATTACK: MIDDLE SECTION FOREFIST PUNCH WHILST MOVING FORWARDS IN WALKING STANCE. START WITH RIGHT HAND/ LEG
DEFENCE: MOVE THE RIGHT OR LEG BACK INTO WALKING STANCE WHILST PERFORMING MIDDLE SECTION INNER FOREARM BLOCK
COUNTER: MIDDLE SECTION FOREFIST PUNCH

EXAMPLE 2
ATTACK: MIDDLE SECTION FOREFIST PUNCH WHILST MOVING FORWARDS IN WAKING STANCE. START WITH RIGHT LEG/ HAND.
DEFENCE: MOVE THE RIGHT OR LEFT LEG BACK IN WALKING STANCE WHILST PERFORMING MIDDLE SECTION OUTER FOREARM BLOCK
COUNTER: MIDDLE SECTION FOREFIST PUNCH

EXAMPLE 3
ATTACK: LOWER SECTION FRONT SNAP KICK WHILST MOVING FORWARDS INTO WALKING STANCE. START WITH RIGHT LEG/
DEFENCE: MOVE THE RIGHT LEG BACK INTO WALKING STANCE WHILST PERFORMING LOWER SECTION OUTER FOREARM BLOCK
COUNTER: MIDDLE SECTION FOREFIST PUNCH

EXAMPLE 4
ATTACK: MIDDLE SECTION FOREFIST PUNCH WHILST MOVING FORWARDS IN WALKING STANCE. START WITH THE RIGHT HAND/ LEG
DEFENCE: STEP BACK INTO L STANCE WITH RIGHT LEG WHILST PERFORMING MIDDLE SECTION INNER FOREARM BLOCK
COUNTER: BRING THE FRONT LEG BACK THEN SLIDE IN PERFORMING MIDDLE SECTION KNIFEHAND SIDE STRIKE

EXAMPLE 5
ATTACK: HIGH SECTION FOREFIST PUNCH WHILST MOVING FORWARDS IN WALKING STANCE. START WITH RIGHT HAND/ LEG.
DEFENCE: MOVE THE RIGHT OR LEFT LEG BACK WHILST PERFORMING HIGH SECTION RISING BLOCK
COUNTER: BRING THE FRONT LEG BACK AND SLIDE FORWARDS WHILST PERFORMINGHIGH SECTION REVERSE KNIFEHAND FRONT STRIKE

TWO STEP SPARRING (IBO MATSOGI)

Two step sparring is the next progression from three step sparring and0 requires the students to combine hand and foot attacks and defences. It is optional whether the attacking student starts with a hand or foot attack. The following are examples of two step sparring:

EXAMPLE 1
ATTACK: STEP FORWARDS IN RIGHT WALKING STANCE PERFORMING MIDDLE SECTION RIGHT FOREFIST PUNCH, THEN STEP FORWARDS IN LEFT WALKING STANCE PERFORMING LEFT FRONT SNAP KICK.
DEFENCE: STEP BACKWARDS WITH RIGHT LEG INTO LEFT WALKING STANCE PERFORMING MIDDLE SECTION LEFT INNER FOREARM BLOCK, THEN STEP BACKWARDS INTO RIGHT WALKING STANCE WHILST PERFORMING RIGHT OUTER FOREARM LOW BLOCK.
COUNTER: MIDDLE SECTION LEFT FOREFIST PUNCH.

EXAMPLE 2
ATTACK: FROM RIGHT L STANCE STEP FORWARDS PERFORMING RIGHT MIDDLE SECTION TURNING KICK, THEN STEP FORWARDS PERFORMING LEFT HIGH SECTION BACKFIST.
DEFENCE: STEP BACKWARDS WITH THE LEFT LEG INTO L STANCE PERFORMING RIGHT INWARDS OUTER FOREARM BLACK, THEN STEP BACKWARDS WITH RIGHT LEG INTO WALKING STANCE WHILST PERFORMING HIGH SECTION OUTER FOREARM BLOCK.
COUNTER: SLIDE FORWARDS WHILST PERFORMING RIGHT REVERSE KNIFEHAND FRONT STRIKE.

EXAMPLE 3
ATTACK: STEP THE RIGHT LEG FOREWARDS INTO LEFT L STANCE WHILST PERFORMING MIDDLE SECTION SIDE PUNCH, THEN LIFT THE LEFT LEG TO PERFORM HIGH SECTION LEFT TURNING KICK TO OPPONENTS HEAD.
DEFENCE: MOVE THE RIGHT LEG BACK INTO L STANCE WHILST PERFORMING MIDDLE SECTION FOREARM GUARDING BLOCK, THEN STEP BACK SLIDING TO THE LEFT MOVING OUT OF RANGE OF TURNING KICK INTO LEFT L STANCE WITH FORAERM GUARDING BLOCK.
COUNTER: PERFORM JUMPING FRONT SNAP KICK USING THE LEFT LEG.

NOTES:
1) BEFORE ATTACK REMEMBER THAT BOTH STUDENTS WUST ACKNOWLEDGE READINESS USING 'KIUP'
2) THE ATTACKER MUST MEASURE UP USING THEIR RIGHT FOOT OT THE OUTSIDE OF THEIR OPPONENT'S LEFT FOOT BEFORE EACH COMBINATION. TO START WITH A KICKING TECHNIQUE THERE MUST BE A HALF FOOT OVERLAP. TO START WITH A PUNCHING TECHNIQUE THERE MUST BE A FULL FOOT OVERLAP.
3) THE DEFENDER MUST FINISH THEIR DEFENCE COMBINATION BY RETURNING TO L STANCE WITH FOREARM GUARDING BLOCK TO SHOW READINESS FOR FUTURE ATTACKS.
4) ALL TECHNIQUES MUST BE ACCOMPANIED BY BREATH CONTROL AND USING SINE WAVE.

5TH KUP

PATTERN YUL GOK

NO. OF MOVEMENTS 38

READY POSITIONS NARANI CHUNBI

C

A ──X── B

E ────────── F

D

DIAGRAM

MEANING OF PATTERN

YUL GOK is the pseudonym of the great philosopher and Scholar Yi I (1536- 1584 AD), nicknamed the 'Confucius of Korea'. The 38 movements represent his birthplace on the 38th degree latitude and the diagram represents 'scholar'.

MOVEMENTS IN PATTERN

STANCES	**SOGI**
WALKING STANCE	GUNNUN SOGI
L STANCE	NIUNJA SOGI
X STANCE	KYOCHA SOGI

BLOCKS	**MAKGI**
HIGH OUTER FOREARM SIDE BLOCK	NAPUNDE BAKAT PALMOK YOP MAKGI
MIDDLE INNER FOREARM BLOCK	KAUNDE AN PALMOK MAKGI
TWIN KNIFEHAND BLOCK	SANG SONKAL MAKGI
HIGH DOUBLE FOREARM BLOCK	NAPUNDE DOO PLAMOK MAKGI
HIGH HOOKING BLOCK	NAPUNDE GOLCHO MAKGI

PUNCHES	**JIRUGI**
MIDDLE PUNCH	KAUNDE JIRUGI

STRIKES	**TAERIGI**
BACK FIST SIDE/BACK STRIKE	DUNG JOOMUK YOPDWI TARIGI
FRONT ELBOW STRIKE	AN PALKUP TAERIGI

THRUST	**TULGI**
MIDDLE STRAIGHT FINGERTIP THRUST	KAUNDE SUN SONKUT TULGI

KICK	**CHAGI**
LOW FRONT SNAP KICK	NAJUNDE AP CHA BUSIGI
MIDDLE SIDE PIERCING KICK	KAUNDE YOP CHA JIRUGI

END	BRING LEFT FOOT BACK TO NARANI JUNBI SOGI

4th KUP

PATTERN   JOONG GUN

NO. OF MOVEMENTS   32

READY POSITION   MOA JUNBI SOGI A

MEANING OF PATTERN

DIAGRAM

JOONG GUN IS NAMED AFTER THE PATRIOT AN OONG GUN WHO ASSASSINATED HIRO BUM0-ITO, THE FIRST JAPANESE GOVERNER GENERAL OF KOREA, KNOWN AS THE MAN WHO PLAYED THE LEADING PART IN THE KOREA/ JAPAN MERGER. THERE ARE 32 MOVEMENTS IN THIS PATTERN TO REPRESENT MR AN'S AGE WHEN HE WAS EXECUTED IN LUI SHUNG PRISON IN 1910.

MOVEMENTS IN PATTERN

STANCES	**SOGI**
WALKING STANCE	GUNNUN SOGI
L STANCE	NIUNJA SOGI
LOW STANCE	NACHUO SOGI
FIXED STANCE	GOJUNG SOGI
CLOSE STANCE	MOA SOGI
REAR FOOT STANCE	DWIT BAL SOGI

BLOCKS	**MAKGI**
PALM PRESSING BLOCK	SONBADAK NOOLLO MAKGI
MIDDLE REVERSE KNIFEHAND SIDE BLOCK	KAUNDE SONKAL DUNG YOP MAKGI
U SHAPED BLOCK	DIGUTCHA MAKGI
PALM UPWARD BLOCK	SONBADAK OLLYO MAKGI
X FIST RISING BLOCK	KYOCHA JOOMUK CHOOKYO MAKGI
HIGH DOUBLE FOREARM BLOCK	NAPUNDE DOOPALMOK MAKGI
MIDDLE KNIFEHAND GUARDING BLOCK	KAUNDE SONKAL DAEBI MAKGI
MIDDLE FOREARM GUARDING BLOCK	KAUNDE BAKAT PALMOK DAEBI MAKGI

PUNCHES	**JIRUGI**
MIDDLE PUNCH	KAUNDE JIRUGI
ANGLE PUNCH	GIOKJA JIRUGI
HIGH PUNCH	NOPUNDE JIRUGI
TWIN FIST UPSET PUNCH	SANG JOOMUK DWIJIBO JIRUGI
HIGH TWIN FIST VERTICAL PUNCH	NOPUNDE SANG JOOMUK SEWO JIRUGI

STRIKE
HIGH BACKFIST SIDE STRIKE
UPPER ELBOW STRIKE

KICK
MIDDLE SIDE PIERCING KICK
LOW FRONT SNAP KICK

RELEASE FROM HOLD
END:

TAERIGI
NAPUNDE DUNG JOOMUK TAERIGI
WI PALKUP TAERIGI

CHAGI
KAUNDE YOP CHA JIRUGI
NAJUNDE AP CHA BUSIGI

JAPP YOSUL TAE
BRING LEFT FOOT BACK TO MOA JUNBI
SOGI A

3RD KUP

PATTERN TOI GYE

NO. OF MOVEMENTS 37

READY POSITION MOA JUNBI SOGI A

```
        C
A ——X—— B

E        F

        D
```

DIAGRAM

MEANING OF PATTERN
TOI GYE IS THE PEN NAME OF THE NOTED SCHOLAR YI HWANG (16TH CENTURY), AN AUTHORITY ON NEO-CONFUCIANISM. THE 37 MOVEMENTS OF THE PATTERN REFER TO HIS BIRTHPLACE ON THE 37TH DEGREE LATTITUDE AND THE DIAGRAM REPRESENTS "SCHOLAR".

MOVEMENTS IN PATTERN

STANCES
WALKING STANCE
L STANCE
SITTING STANCE
CLOSE STANCE
X STANCE

SOGI
GUNNUN SOGI
NIUNJA SOGI
ANNUN SOGI
MOA SOGI
KYOCHA SOGI

BLOCKS
LOW OUTER FOREARM BLOCK
MIDDLE INNER FOREARM BLOCK
X FIST PRESSING BLOCK
OUTER FOREARM W SHAPED BLOCK
LOW DOUBLE FOREARM PUSHING BLOCK
LOW KNIFEHAND GUARDING BLOCK
HIGH DOUBLE FOREARM BLOCK
MIDDLE KNIFEHAND GUARDING BLOCK
INNER FOREARM CIRCULAR BLOCK

MAKGI
NAJUNDE BAKAT PALMOK MAKGI
KAUNDE AN PALMOK MAKGI
KYOCHA JOOMUK NOOLLO MAKGI
BAKAT PALMOK SAN MAKGI
NAJUNDE DOO PALMOK MIRO MAKGI
NAJUNDE SONKAL DAEBI MAKGI
NAPUNDE DOO PALMOK MAKGI
KAUNDE SONKAL DAEBI MAKGI
AN PLAMOK DOLIMYO MAKGI

PUNCHES
MIDDLE PUNCH
HIGHTWIN FIST
VERTICAL PUNCH

JIRUGI
KAUNDE JIRUGI
NAPUNDE SANG JOOMUK SEWO JIRUGI

STRIKE
BACK FIST SIDE/ BACK STRIKE
BACK FIST SIDE
STRIKE

THRUST
LOW UPSET FINGERTIP THRUST
HIGH FLAT FINGERTIP THRUST

KICK
MIDDLE FONT SNAP KICK
LOW SIDE FRONT SNAP KICK
KNEE UPWARD KICK

END:

TAERIGI
DUNG JOOMUK YOPDWI TAERIGI
NAPUNDE DUNG JOOMUK YOP
TAERIGI

TULGI
NAJUNDE DWIJIBO SONKUT TULGI
NAPUNDE OPUN SONKUT TULGI

CHAGI
KAUNDE AP CHA BUSIGI
NAJUNDE YOP/ AP CHA BUSIGI
MOORUP OLLYO CHAGI

BRING RIGHT FOOT BACK TO MOA
SOGI B

2ND KUP

PATTERN   HWA RANG

NO. OF MOVEMENTS 29

READY POSITION   MOA JUNBI SOGI C

```
              C
A ──────X────── B


    DIAGRAM
  E ──────── F
         D
```

DIAGRAM

MEANING OF PATTERN

HWA RANG IS NAMED AFTER THE HWARANG YOUTH GROUP WHICH ORIGINTED IN THE SILLA DYNASTY IN THE EARLY 7TH CENTURY. THE 29 MOVEMENTS REFER TO THE 29TH INFANTRY DIVISION WHERE TAEKWONDO DEVELOPED INTO MATURITY.

MOVEMENTS IN PATTERN

STANCES
WALKING STANCE
L STANCE
SITTING STANCE
CLOSE STANCE
VERTICAL STANCE
FIXED STANCE

SOGI
GUNNUN SOGI
NIUNJA SOGI
ANNUN SOGI
MOA SOGI
SOOJIK SOGI
GOJUNG SOGI

BLOCKS
LOW OUTER FOREARM BLOCK
TWIN FOREARM BLOCK
X FIST PRESSING BLOCK
HIGH SIDE/ FRONT INNER
FOREARM BLOCK
MIDDLE KNIFEHAND GUARDING
BLOCK
PALM PUSHING BLOCK

MAKGI
NAJUNDE BAKAT PALMOK MAKGI
SANG PALMOK MAKGI
KYOCHA JOOMUK NOOLLO MAKGI
NAPUNDE YOP/ AP AN
PALMOK MAKGI
KAUNDE SONKAL DAEBI
MAKGI
SONBADAK MIRO MAKGI

PUNCHES
MIDDLE PUNCH
UPWARDS PUNCH

JIRUGI
KAUNDE JIRUGI
OLLYO JIRUGI

STRIKE
DOWNWARD KNIFEHAND STRIKE
MIDDLE KNIFEHAND SIDE STRIKE

THRUST
STRAIGHT FINGERTIP THRUST
SIDE ELBOW THRUST

KICK
MIDDLE SIDE PIERCING KICK
HIGH TURNING KICK

END:

TAERIGI
NAERYO SONKAL TAERIGI
KAUNDE SONKAL YOP TAERIGI

TULGI
SUN SONKUT TULGI
YOP PALKUP TULGI

CHAGI
KAUNDE YOP CHA JIRUGI
NOPUNDE DOLLYO CHAGI

BRING RIGHT FOOT BACK TO MOA JUNBI
SOGI C

1ST KUP

PATTERN   CHOONG MOO

NO. OF MOVEMENTS   30

READY POSITION   NARANI JUNBI SOGI

MEANING OF PATTERN
CHOONG MOO WAS THE NAME
GIVEN TO THE GREAT ADMIRAL YI
SUN-SIN OF THE YI DYNASTY. HE WAS REPUTED
TO HAVE INVENTED THE FIRST ARMOURED BATTLESHIP (KOBUKSON) IN
1592, WHICH WAS THE PRECURSOR OF THE PRESENT DAY SUBMARINE. THE
REASON WHY THIS PATTERN END WITH A LEFT HANDED ATTACK IS TO
SYMBOLISE HIS REGRETTABLE DEATH, HAVING NO CHANCE TO SHOW HIS
UNRESTRAINED POTENTIALITY, CHECKED BY THE FORCED RESERVATION OF
HIS LOYALTY TO THE KING

DIAGRAM

```
              C
  A ——————X—————— B
          |
          |
  E ——————D—————— F
```

MOVEMENTS IN PATTERN

STANCES
WALKING STANCE
L STANCE
SITTING STANCE
BENDING READY STANCE A

SOGI
GUNNUN SOGI
NIUNJA SOGI
ANNUN SOGI
GOBURYO JUNBI SOGI A

BLOCKS
LOW OUTER FOREARM BLOCK
TWIN KNIFEHAND BLOCK
U SHAPED BLOCK
MIDDLE OUTER FOREARM FRONT
BLOCK
DOUBLE PALM UPWARD BLOCK
OUTER FOREARM RISING BLOCK
MIDDLE X KNIFEHAND BLOCK
HIGH DOUBLE FOREARM BLOCK
MIDDLE KNIFEHAND GUARDING
BLOCK
MIDDLE OUTER FOREARM
GUARDING BLOCK

MAKGI
NAJUNDE BAKAT PALMOK MAKGI
SANG SONKAL MAKGI
DIGUTCHA MAKGI
KAUNDE BAKAT PALMOK AP
MAKGI
DOO SONBADAK OLLYO MAKGI
BAKAT PALMOK CHOOKYO MAKGI
KAUNDE KYOCHA SONKAL MAKGI
NAPUNDE DOO PALMOK MAKGI
KAUNDE SONKAL DAEBI
MAKGI
KAUNDE BAKAT PALMOK DAEBI
MAKGI

PUNCHES
MIDDLE PUNCH

JIRUGI
KAUNDE JIRUGI

STRIKE
BACKFIST SIDE/ BACK STRIKE
HIGH REVERSE KNIFEHAND
FRONT STRIKE
HIGH BACKFIST SIDE STRIKE
HIGH KNIFEHAND FRONT
STRIKE

THRUST
LOW UPSET FINGERTIP THRUST
HIGH FLAT FINGERTIP THRUST
MIDDLE FLAT FINGERTIP
THRUST

KICK
MIDDLE SIDE PIERCING KICK
FLYING SIDE PIERCING KICK
KNEE UPWARD KICK
HIGH TURNING KICK
MIDDLE BACK PIERCING KICK

END:

TAERIGI
DUNG JOOMUK YOPDWI TAERIGI
NAPUNDE SONKAL DUNG
AP TAERIGI
NAPUNDE DUNG JOOMUK TAERIGI
NAPUNDE SONKAL AP
TAERIGI

TULGI
NAJUNDE DWIJIBO SONKUT TULGI
NAPUNDE OPUN SONKUT TULGI
KAUNDE SUN SONKUT
TULGI

CHAGI
KAUNDE YOP CHA JIRUGI
TWIMYO YOP CHA JIRUGI
MOORUP OLLYO CHAGI
NAPUNDE DOLLYO CHAGI
KAUNDE DWITCHA JIRUGI

BRING LEFT FOOT BACKTO NARANI
JUNBI SOGI

NOTES

C.O.D.E
COMBAT ARTS

C.O.D.E
MMA

C.O.D.E
TAEKWONDO

CODE Combat Arts | CODE
Taekwon-Do
Classes in South Cambs
www.codecombatarts.co.uk
codecombatarts@gmail.com
07825559642

18864597R00024

Printed in Great Britain
by Amazon